Mel Bay Presents

More Songs for HARMONICA

By William Bay

1 2 3 4 5 6 7 8 9 0

© 1990 BY MEL BAY PUBLICATIONS, INC., PACIFIC, MO.
INTERNATIONAL COPYRIGHT SECURED. ALL RIGHTS RESERVED. PRINTED IN U.S.A.

CONTENTS

America 10	Marines' Hymn 12
America the Beautiful 8	The Mulligan Guard 30
The British Grenadiers 17	My Home's Across the Smokey Mountains . 25
The Caissons 28	Once There Were Three Fisherman 22
Comin' Through the Rye 15	Praise Him in the Morning 5
Everybody Loves Saturday Night 19	Putting on the Style 27
Eyes of Texas 9	Railroad Bill 6
Father's Whiskers 23	Raise a Ruckus Tonight 24
For He's a Jolly Good Fellow 14	Rise & Shine 26
Give Me Oil in My Lamp 13	Rock of Ages 7
Goin' Down the Road Feelin' Bad 18	Rock-A-My Soul 20
Hey Lolly 22	Swanee River 21
I Know Where I'm Goin' 16	Ten Thousand Miles 11
The Keeper 29	This Little Light of Mine 32
Lolly Too Dum 31	The Wearin' of the Green 4

Diatonic Note Chart 3

DIATONIC NOTE CHART

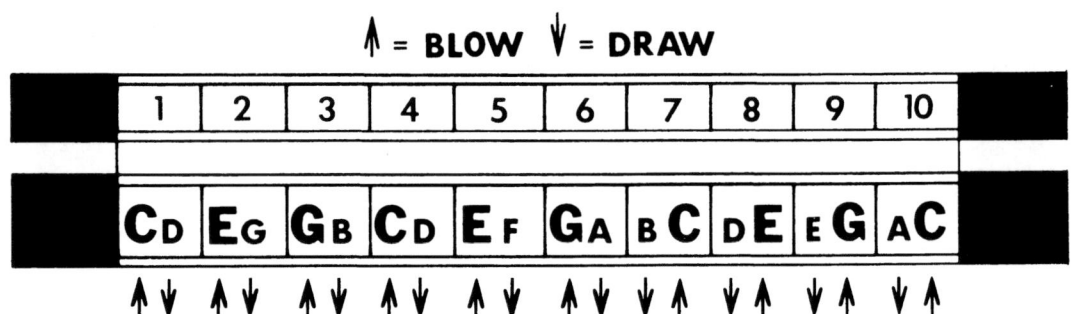

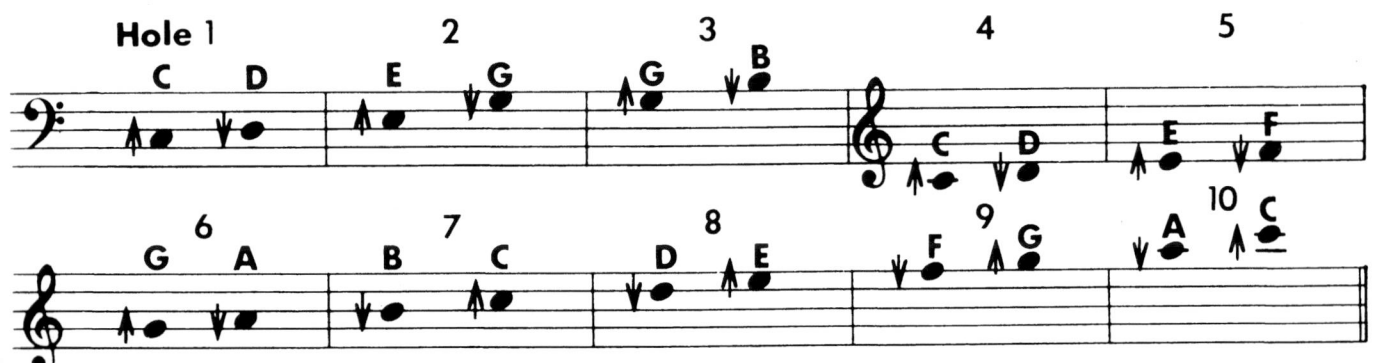

THE WEARIN' OF THE GREEN

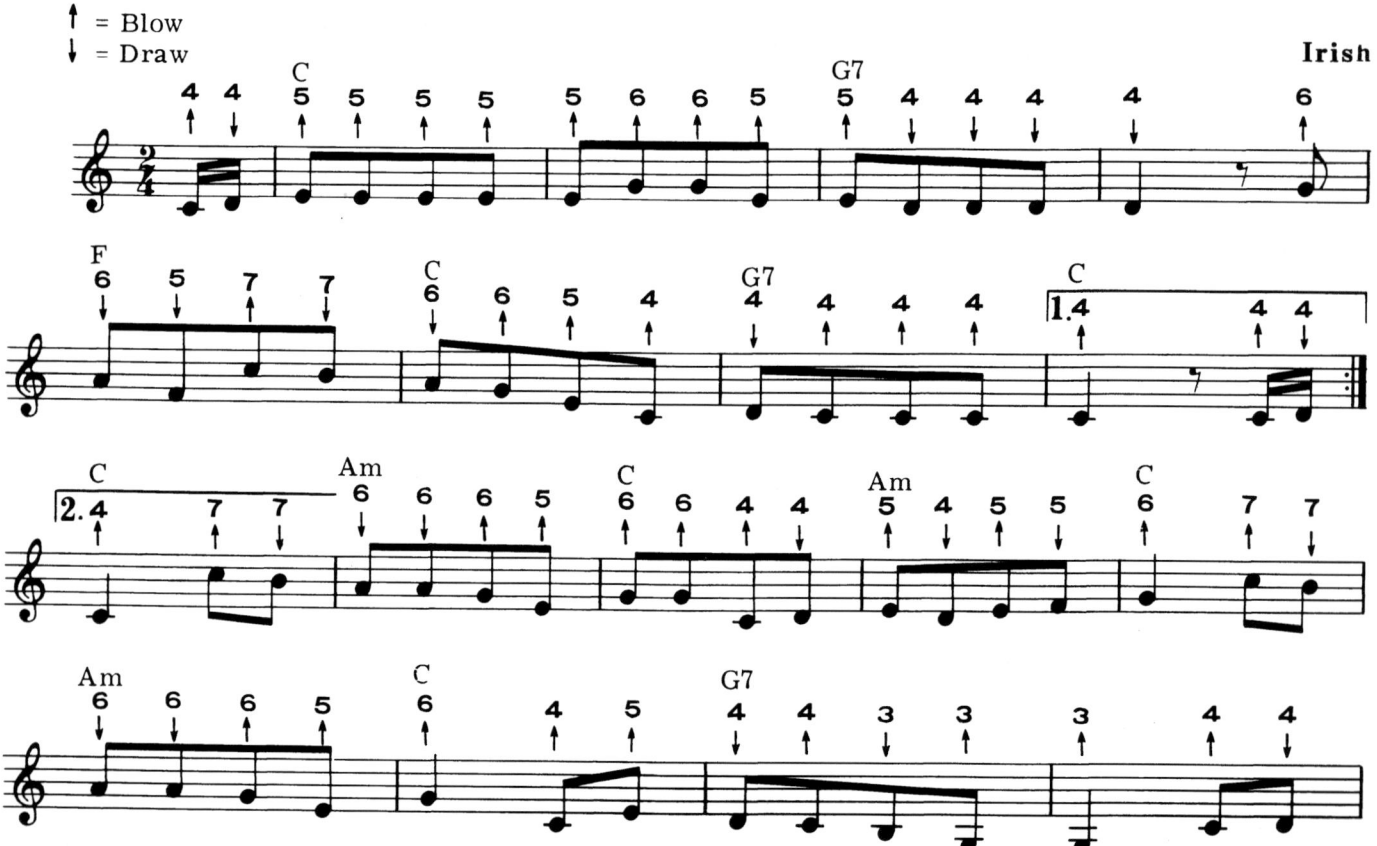

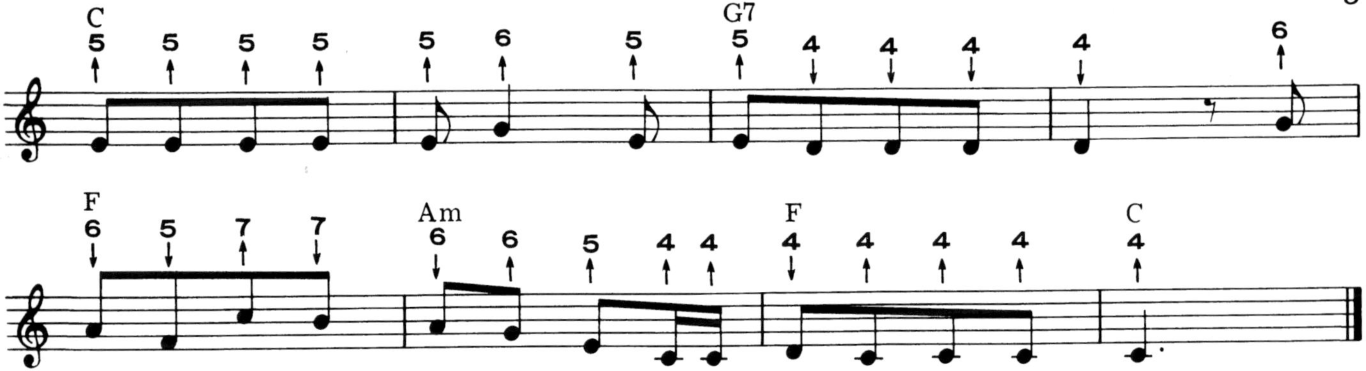

PRAISE HIM IN THE MORNING

↑ = Blow
↓ = Draw

Gospel Song

RAILROAD BILL

ROCK OF AGES

AMERICA THE BEAUTIFUL

EYES OF TEXAS

AMERICA

MARINES' HYMN

GIVE ME OIL IN MY LAMP

COMIN' THROUGH THE RYE

I KNOW WHERE I'M GOIN'

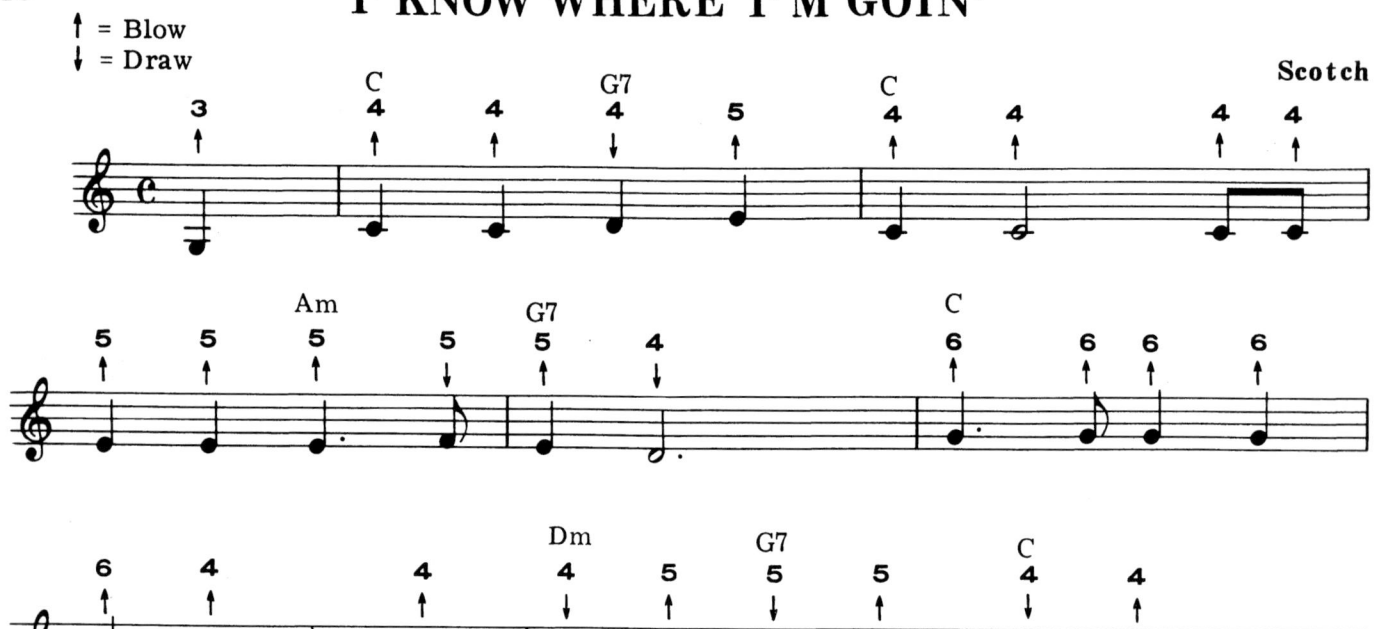

THE BRITISH GRENADIERS

EVERYBODY LOVES SATURDAY NIGHT

ROCK-A-MY SOUL

SWANEE RIVER

HEY LOLLY

↑ = Blow
↓ = Draw

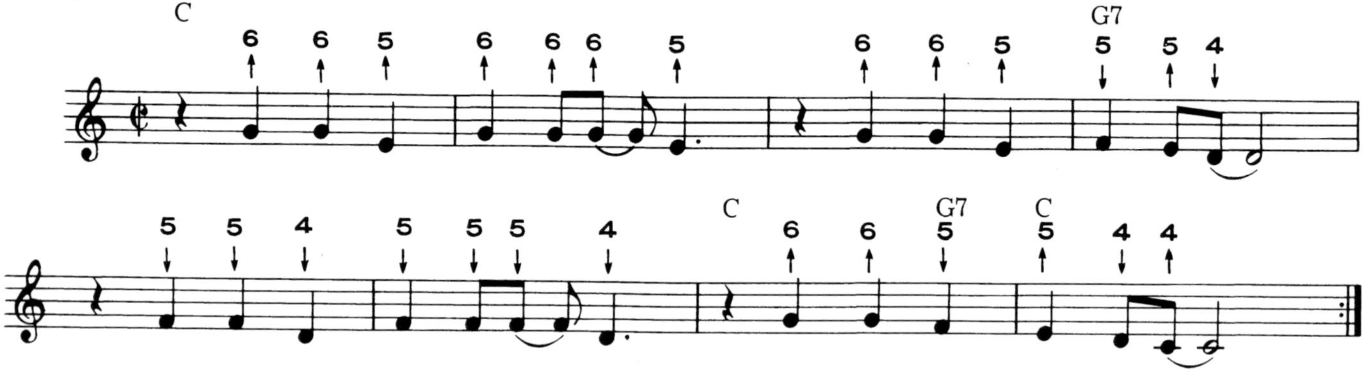

ONCE THERE WERE THREE FISHERMAN

↑ = Blow
↓ = Draw

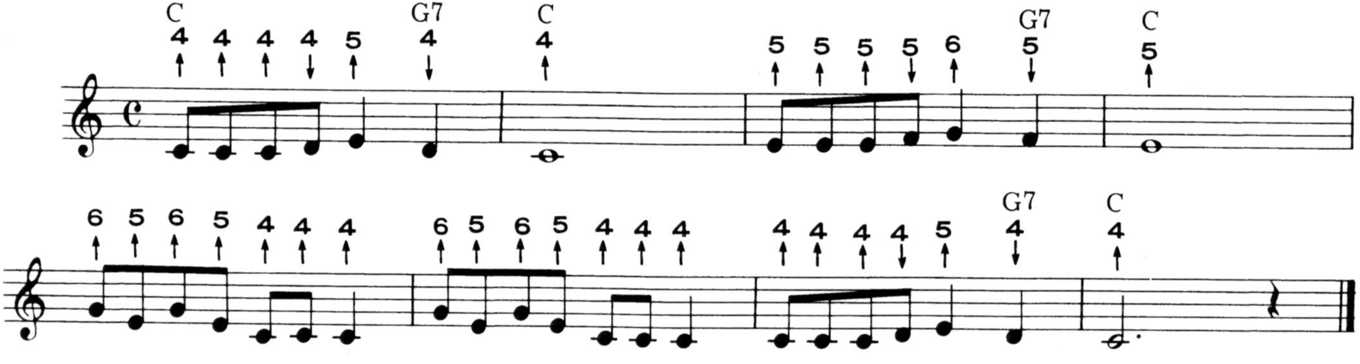

FATHER'S WHISKERS

American Folk Song

RAISE A RUCKUS TONIGHT

↑ = Blow
↓ = Draw

MY HOME'S ACROSS THE SMOKEY MOUNTAINS

PUTTING ON THE STYLE

THE CAISSONS

THE KEEPER

THE MULLIGAN GUARD

LOLLY TOO DUM

THIS LITTLE LIGHT OF MINE